# Password Book

Belongs to:

_____

D1414168

# Password writing tips

1. Avoid using the same password for multiple websites/apps. This will prevent anyone who's gained access to one of your passwords from also accessing other sites

2. Use a combination of capital and lowercase letters, and consider adding in special characters for more strength

3. Avoid writing passwords in full. Instead, leave out several characters and include a hint in the notes area. For example, if your password is 'dAffodil123', write it down as *A*****l*2*, and in the notes area write down 'name of flower'

Note: This is a simple example of how you can keep your passwords safe. Use your creativity to come up with additional steps to ensure more security

Website: _____

Username: _____

Password: _____

Notes: _____

_____

_____

Website: _____

Username: _____

Password: _____

Notes: _____

_____

_____

Website: _____

Username: _____

Password: _____

Notes: _____

_____

_____

Website: _____

Username: _____

Password: _____

Notes: _____

_____

_____

B C D E F G H I J K L M N O P Q R S T U V W X Y Z

**A**

B
C
D
E
F
G

Website: _____
Username: _____
Password: _____
Notes: _____
_____
_____

H
I
J
K
L
M

Website: _____
Username: _____
Password: _____
Notes: _____
_____
_____

N
O
P
Q
R
S
T

Website: _____
Username: _____
Password: _____
Notes: _____
_____
_____

U
V
W
X
Y
Z

Website: _____
Username: _____
Password: _____
Notes: _____
_____
_____

Website: _____
Username: _____
Password: _____
Notes: _____
_____
_____

Website: _____
Username: _____
Password: _____
Notes: _____
_____
_____

Website: _____
Username: _____
Password: _____
Notes: _____
_____
_____

Website: _____
Username: _____
Password: _____
Notes: _____
_____
_____

**A**
B
C
D
E
F
G

Website: _____
Username: _____
Password: _____
Notes: _____
_____
_____

H
I
J
K
L
M

Website: _____
Username: _____
Password: _____
Notes: _____
_____
_____

N
O
P
Q
R
S

Website: _____
Username: _____
Password: _____
Notes: _____
_____
_____

T
U
V
W
X
Y
Z

Website: _____
Username: _____
Password: _____
Notes: _____
_____
_____

Website: _____

Username: _____

Password: _____

Notes: _____

_____

_____

_____

Website: _____

Username: _____

Password: _____

Notes: _____

_____

_____

_____

Website: _____

Username: _____

Password: _____

Notes: _____

_____

_____

_____

Website: _____

Username: _____

Password: _____

Notes: _____

_____

_____

_____

A
B
C
D
E
F
G
H
I
J
K
L
M
N
O
P
Q
R
S
T
U
V
W
X
Y
Z

A
**B**
C
D
E
F
G
H
I
J
K
L
M
N
O
P
Q
R
S
T
U
V
W
X
Y
Z

Website: _____
Username: _____
Password: _____
Notes: _____
_____
_____

Website: _____
Username: _____
Password: _____
Notes: _____
_____
_____

Website: _____
Username: _____
Password: _____
Notes: _____
_____
_____

Website: _____
Username: _____
Password: _____
Notes: _____
_____
_____

Website: _____

Username: _____

Password: _____

Notes: _____

_____

_____

Website: _____

Username: _____

Password: _____

Notes: _____

_____

_____

Website: _____

Username: _____

Password: _____

Notes: _____

_____

_____

Website: _____

Username: _____

Password: _____

Notes: _____

_____

_____

A
B
C
D
E
F
G
H
I
J
K
L
M
N
O
P
Q
R
S
T
U
V
W
X
Y
Z

A
**B**
C
D
E
F
G
H
I
J
K
L
M
N
O
P
Q
R
S
T
U
V
W
X
Y
Z

Website: _____

Username: _____

Password: _____

Notes: _____

_____

_____

Website: _____

Username: _____

Password: _____

Notes: _____

_____

_____

Website: _____

Username: _____

Password: _____

Notes: _____

_____

_____

Website: _____

Username: _____

Password: _____

Notes: _____

_____

_____

Website: _____

Username: _____

Password: _____

Notes: _____

_____

_____

Website: _____

Username: _____

Password: _____

Notes: _____

_____

_____

Website: _____

Username: _____

Password: _____

Notes: _____

_____

_____

Website: _____

Username: _____

Password: _____

Notes: _____

_____

_____

A
B
**C**
D
E
F
G
H
I
J
K
L
M
N
O
P
Q
R
S
T
U
V
W
X
Y
Z

A
B
**C**
D
E
F
G
H
I
J
K
L
M
N
O
P
Q
R
S
T
U
V
W
X
Y
Z

Website: _____

Username: _____

Password: _____

Notes: _____

_____

_____

Website: _____

Username: _____

Password: _____

Notes: _____

_____

_____

Website: _____

Username: _____

Password: _____

Notes: _____

_____

_____

Website: _____

Username: _____

Password: _____

Notes: _____

_____

_____

Website: _____

Username: _____

Password: _____

Notes: _____

_____

_____

Website: _____

Username: _____

Password: _____

Notes: _____

_____

_____

Website: _____

Username: _____

Password: _____

Notes: _____

_____

_____

Website: _____

Username: _____

Password: _____

Notes: _____

_____

_____

A
B
C
D
E
F
G
H
I
J
K
L
M
N
O
P
Q
R
S
T
U
V
W
X
Y
Z

A
B
**C**
D
E
F

Website: _____
Username: _____
Password: _____
Notes: _____
_____
_____

G
H
I
J
K
L
M

Website: _____
Username: _____
Password: _____
Notes: _____
_____
_____

N
O
P
Q
R
S
T

Website: _____
Username: _____
Password: _____
Notes: _____
_____
_____

U
V
W
X
Y
Z

Website: _____
Username: _____
Password: _____
Notes: _____
_____
_____

Website: _____

Username: _____

Password: _____

Notes: _____

_____

_____

Website: _____

Username: _____

Password: _____

Notes: _____

_____

_____

Website: _____

Username: _____

Password: _____

Notes: _____

_____

_____

Website: _____

Username: _____

Password: _____

Notes: _____

_____

_____

A
B
C
**D**
E
F
G
H
I
J
K
L
M
N
O
P
Q
R
S
T
U
V
W
X
Y
Z

A
B
C
**D**
E
F
G
H
I
J
K
L
M
N
O
P
Q
R
S
T
U
V
W
X
Y
Z

Website: _____

Username: _____

Password: _____

Notes: _____

_____

_____

Website: _____

Username: _____

Password: _____

Notes: _____

_____

_____

Website: _____

Username: _____

Password: _____

Notes: _____

_____

_____

Website: _____

Username: _____

Password: _____

Notes: _____

_____

_____

Website: _____

Username: _____

Password: _____

Notes: _____

_____

_____

Website: _____

Username: _____

Password: _____

Notes: _____

_____

_____

Website: _____

Username: _____

Password: _____

Notes: _____

_____

_____

Website: _____

Username: _____

Password: _____

Notes: _____

_____

_____

A
B
C
D
E
F
G
H
I
J
K
L
M
N
O
P
Q
R
S
T
U
V
W
X
Y
Z

A
B
C
**D**
E
F

Website: _____
Username: _____
Password: _____
Notes: _____
_____
_____

G
H
I
J
K
L
M

Website: _____
Username: _____
Password: _____
Notes: _____
_____
_____

N
O
P
Q
R
S
T

Website: _____
Username: _____
Password: _____
Notes: _____
_____
_____

U
V
W
X
Y
Z

Website: _____
Username: _____
Password: _____
Notes: _____
_____
_____

Website: _____

Username: _____

Password: _____

Notes: _____

_____

_____

Website: _____

Username: _____

Password: _____

Notes: _____

_____

_____

Website: _____

Username: _____

Password: _____

Notes: _____

_____

_____

Website: _____

Username: _____

Password: _____

Notes: _____

_____

_____

A
B
C
D
**E**
F
G
H
I
J
K
L
M
N
O
P
Q
R
S
T
U
V
W
X
Y
Z

A
B
C
D
**E**
F
G
H
I
J
K
L
M
N
O
P
Q
R
S
T
U
V
W
X
Y
Z

Website: _____

Username: _____

Password: _____

Notes: _____

_____

_____

Website: _____

Username: _____

Password: _____

Notes: _____

_____

_____

Website: _____

Username: _____

Password: _____

Notes: _____

_____

_____

Website: _____

Username: _____

Password: _____

Notes: _____

_____

_____

Website: _____

Username: _____

Password: _____

Notes: _____

_____

_____

Website: _____

Username: _____

Password: _____

Notes: _____

_____

_____

Website: _____

Username: _____

Password: _____

Notes: _____

_____

_____

Website: _____

Username: _____

Password: _____

Notes: _____

_____

_____

A
B
C
D
**E**
F
G
H
I
J
K
L
M
N
O
P
Q
R
S
T
U
V
W
X
Y
Z

A
B
C
D
**E**
F
G
H
I
J
K
L
M
N
O
P
Q
R
S
T
U
V
W
X
Y
Z

Website: _____
Username: _____
Password: _____
Notes: _____
_____
_____

Website: _____
Username: _____
Password: _____
Notes: _____
_____
_____

Website: _____
Username: _____
Password: _____
Notes: _____
_____
_____

Website: _____
Username: _____
Password: _____
Notes: _____
_____
_____

Website: _____

Username: _____

Password: _____

Notes: _____

_____

_____

Website: _____

Username: _____

Password: _____

Notes: _____

_____

_____

Website: _____

Username: _____

Password: _____

Notes: _____

_____

_____

Website: _____

Username: _____

Password: _____

Notes: _____

_____

_____

A
B
C
D
E
**F**
G
H
I
J
K
L
M
N
O
P
Q
R
S
T
U
V
W
X
Y
Z

A B C D E **F** G H I J K L M N O P Q R S T U V W X Y Z

Website: _____
Username: _____
Password: _____
Notes: _____
_____
_____

Website: _____
Username: _____
Password: _____
Notes: _____
_____
_____

Website: _____
Username: _____
Password: _____
Notes: _____
_____
_____

Website: _____
Username: _____
Password: _____
Notes: _____
_____
_____

Website: _____
Username: _____
Password: _____
Notes: _____
_____
_____

Website: _____
Username: _____
Password: _____
Notes: _____
_____
_____

Website: _____
Username: _____
Password: _____
Notes: _____
_____
_____

Website: _____
Username: _____
Password: _____
Notes: _____
_____
_____

A
B
C
D
E
**F**
G
H
I
J
K
L
M
N
O
P
Q
R
S
T
U
V
W
X
Y
Z

A
B
C
D
E
**F**
G
H
I
J
K
L
M
N
O
P
Q
R
S
T
U
V
W
X
Y
Z

Website: _____
Username: _____
Password: _____
Notes: _____
_____
_____

Website: _____
Username: _____
Password: _____
Notes: _____
_____
_____

Website: _____
Username: _____
Password: _____
Notes: _____
_____
_____

Website: _____
Username: _____
Password: _____
Notes: _____
_____
_____

Website: _____

Username: _____

Password: _____

Notes: _____

_____

_____

Website: _____

Username: _____

Password: _____

Notes: _____

_____

_____

Website: _____

Username: _____

Password: _____

Notes: _____

_____

_____

Website: _____

Username: _____

Password: _____

Notes: _____

_____

_____

A
B
C
D
E
F
**G**
H
I
J
K
L
M
N
O
P
Q
R
S
T
U
V
W
X
Y
Z

A
B
C
D
E
F

**G**

H
I
J
K
L
M
N
O
P
Q
R
S
T
U
V
W
X
Y
Z

Website: _____

Username: _____

Password: _____

Notes: _____

_____

_____

Website: _____

Username: _____

Password: _____

Notes: _____

_____

_____

Website: _____

Username: _____

Password: _____

Notes: _____

_____

_____

Website: _____

Username: _____

Password: _____

Notes: _____

_____

_____

Website: _____

Username: _____

Password: _____

Notes: _____

_____

_____

Website: _____

Username: _____

Password: _____

Notes: _____

_____

_____

Website: _____

Username: _____

Password: _____

Notes: _____

_____

_____

Website: _____

Username: _____

Password: _____

Notes: _____

_____

_____

A
B
C
D
E
F
G
H
I
J
K
L
M
N
O
P
Q
R
S
T
U
V
W
X
Y
Z

A
B
C
D
E
F
**G**
H
I
J
K
L
M
N
O
P
Q
R
S
T
U
V
W
X
Y
Z

Website: _____
Username: _____
Password: _____
Notes: _____
_____
_____

Website: _____
Username: _____
Password: _____
Notes: _____
_____
_____

Website: _____
Username: _____
Password: _____
Notes: _____
_____
_____

Website: _____
Username: _____
Password: _____
Notes: _____
_____
_____

Website: _____
Username: _____
Password: _____
Notes: _____
_____
_____

Website: _____
Username: _____
Password: _____
Notes: _____
_____
_____

Website: _____
Username: _____
Password: _____
Notes: _____
_____
_____

Website: _____
Username: _____
Password: _____
Notes: _____
_____
_____

A
B
C
D
E
F
G
**H**
I
J
K
L
M
N
O
P
Q
R
S
T
U
V
W
X
Y
Z

A
B Website: _____
C Username: _____
  Password: _____
D Notes: _____
E _____
F _____

G
**H** Website: _____
I Username: _____
  Password: _____
J Notes: _____
K _____
L _____
M

N Website: _____
O Username: _____
  Password: _____
P Notes: _____
Q _____
R _____
S

T Website: _____
U Username: _____
  Password: _____
V Notes: _____
W _____
X _____
Y _____
Z

Website: _____

Username: _____

Password: _____

Notes: _____

_____

_____

Website: _____

Username: _____

Password: _____

Notes: _____

_____

_____

Website: _____

Username: _____

Password: _____

Notes: _____

_____

_____

Website: _____

Username: _____

Password: _____

Notes: _____

_____

_____

A
B
C
D
E
F
G
H
I
J
K
L
M
N
O
P
Q
R
S
T
U
V
W
X
Y
Z

A
B    Website: _____
C    Username: _____
D    Password: _____
     Notes: _____
E    _____
F    _____
G

**H**    Website: _____
     Username: _____
I    Password: _____
J    Notes: _____
K
L    _____
M    _____

N    Website: _____
O    Username: _____
P    Password: _____
Q    Notes: _____
R    _____
S    _____
T

U    Website: _____
V    Username: _____
W    Password: _____
     Notes: _____
X    _____
Y    _____
Z

Website: _____
Username: _____
Password: _____
Notes: _____
_____
_____

Website: _____
Username: _____
Password: _____
Notes: _____
_____
_____

Website: _____
Username: _____
Password: _____
Notes: _____
_____
_____

Website: _____
Username: _____
Password: _____
Notes: _____
_____
_____

A
B
C
D
E
F
G
H
I
J
K
L
M
N
O
P
Q
R
S
T
U
V
W
X
Y
Z

A
B
C
D
E
F
G
H
I
J
K
L
M
N
O
P
Q
R
S
T
U
V
W
X
Y
Z

Website: _____
Username: _____
Password: _____
Notes: _____
_____
_____

Website: _____
Username: _____
Password: _____
Notes: _____
_____
_____

Website: _____
Username: _____
Password: _____
Notes: _____
_____
_____

Website: _____
Username: _____
Password: _____
Notes: _____
_____
_____

Website: _____
Username: _____
Password: _____
Notes: _____
_____
_____

Website: _____
Username: _____
Password: _____
Notes: _____
_____
_____

Website: _____
Username: _____
Password: _____
Notes: _____
_____
_____

Website: _____
Username: _____
Password: _____
Notes: _____
_____
_____

A
B
C
D
E
F
G
H
I
J
K
L
M
N
O
P
Q
R
S
T
U
V
W
X
Y
Z

A B C D E F G H **I** J K L M N O P Q R S T U V W X Y Z

Website: _____
Username: _____
Password: _____
Notes: _____
_____
_____

Website: _____
Username: _____
Password: _____
Notes: _____
_____
_____

Website: _____
Username: _____
Password: _____
Notes: _____
_____
_____

Website: _____
Username: _____
Password: _____
Notes: _____
_____
_____

Website: _____

Username: _____

Password: _____

Notes: _____

_____

_____

Website: _____

Username: _____

Password: _____

Notes: _____

_____

_____

Website: _____

Username: _____

Password: _____

Notes: _____

_____

_____

Website: _____

Username: _____

Password: _____

Notes: _____

_____

_____

A
B
C
D
E
F
G
H
I
J
K
L
M
N
O
P
Q
R
S
T
U
V
W
X
Y
Z

A
B        Website: _____
C        Username: _____
D        Password: _____
E        Notes: _____
F        _____
G        _____

H        Website: _____
I        Username: _____
J        Password: _____
K        Notes: _____
L        _____
M        _____

N        Website: _____
O        Username: _____
P        Password: _____
Q        Notes: _____
R        _____
S        _____

T        Website: _____
U        Username: _____
V        Password: _____
W        Notes: _____
X        _____
Y        _____
Z

Website: _____

Username: _____

Password: _____

Notes: _____

_____

_____

Website: _____

Username: _____

Password: _____

Notes: _____

_____

_____

Website: _____

Username: _____

Password: _____

Notes: _____

_____

_____

Website: _____

Username: _____

Password: _____

Notes: _____

_____

_____

A
B
C
D
E
F
G
H
I
J
K
L
M
N
O
P
Q
R
S
T
U
V
W
X
Y
Z

A
B Website: _____
C Username: _____
D Password: _____
E Notes: _____
F _____
G _____

H Website: _____
I Username: _____
**J** Password: _____
K Notes: _____
L _____
M _____

N Website: _____
O Username: _____
P Password: _____
Q Notes: _____
R _____
S _____

T Website: _____
U Username: _____
V Password: _____
W Notes: _____
X _____
Y _____
Z

Website: _____

Username: _____

Password: _____

Notes: _____

_____

_____

Website: _____

Username: _____

Password: _____

Notes: _____

_____

_____

Website: _____

Username: _____

Password: _____

Notes: _____

_____

_____

Website: _____

Username: _____

Password: _____

Notes: _____

_____

_____

A
B
C
D
E
F
G
H
I
J
**K**
L
M
N
O
P
Q
R
S
T
U
V
W
X
Y
Z

A
B Website: _____
C Username: _____
  Password: _____
D Notes: _____
E _____
F _____
G ━━━━━━━━━━━━━━━━━━━━━━━━━━━
H Website: _____
I Username: _____
J Password: _____
**K** Notes: _____
L _____
M _____
N ━━━━━━━━━━━━━━━━━━━━━━━━━━━
  Website: _____
O Username: _____
P Password: _____
Q Notes: _____
R _____
S _____
T ━━━━━━━━━━━━━━━━━━━━━━━━━━━
  Website: _____
U Username: _____
V Password: _____
W Notes: _____
X _____
Y _____
Z

Website: _____

Username: _____

Password: _____

Notes: _____

_____

_____

Website: _____

Username: _____

Password: _____

Notes: _____

_____

_____

Website: _____

Username: _____

Password: _____

Notes: _____

_____

_____

Website: _____

Username: _____

Password: _____

Notes: _____

_____

_____

A
B
C
D
E
F
G
H
I
J
**K**
L
M
N
O
P
Q
R
S
T
U
V
W
X
Y
Z

A
B
C
D
E
F
G
H
I
J
**K**
L
M
N
O
P
Q
R
S
T
U
V
W
X
Y
Z

Website: _____
Username: _____
Password: _____
Notes: _____
_____
_____

Website: _____
Username: _____
Password: _____
Notes: _____
_____
_____

Website: _____
Username: _____
Password: _____
Notes: _____
_____
_____

Website: _____
Username: _____
Password: _____
Notes: _____
_____
_____

Website: _____

Username: _____

Password: _____

Notes: _____

_____

_____

Website: _____

Username: _____

Password: _____

Notes: _____

_____

_____

Website: _____

Username: _____

Password: _____

Notes: _____

_____

_____

Website: _____

Username: _____

Password: _____

Notes: _____

_____

_____

A
B
C
D
E
F
G
H
I
J
K
L
M
N
O
P
Q
R
S
T
U
V
W
X
Y
Z

A
B Website: _____
C Username: _____
D Password: _____
E Notes: _____
F _____
G _____
H Website: _____
I Username: _____
J Password: _____
K Notes: _____
L _____
M _____
N Website: _____
O Username: _____
P Password: _____
Q Notes: _____
R _____
S _____
T Website: _____
U Username: _____
V Password: _____
W Notes: _____
X _____
Y _____
Z

Website: _____

Username: _____

Password: _____

Notes: _____

_____

_____

Website: _____

Username: _____

Password: _____

Notes: _____

_____

_____

Website: _____

Username: _____

Password: _____

Notes: _____

_____

_____

Website: _____

Username: _____

Password: _____

Notes: _____

_____

_____

A
B
C
D
E
F
G
H
I
J
K
L
M
N
O
P
Q
R
S
T
U
V
W
X
Y
Z

A
B
C
D
E
F
G
H
I
J
K
**L**
M
N
O
P
Q
R
S
T
U
V
W
X
Y
Z

Website: _____

Username: _____

Password: _____

Notes: _____

_____

_____

Website: _____

Username: _____

Password: _____

Notes: _____

_____

_____

Website: _____

Username: _____

Password: _____

Notes: _____

_____

_____

Website: _____

Username: _____

Password: _____

Notes: _____

_____

_____

Website: _____
Username: _____
Password: _____
Notes: _____
_____
_____
_____

Website: _____
Username: _____
Password: _____
Notes: _____
_____
_____
_____

Website: _____
Username: _____
Password: _____
Notes: _____
_____
_____
_____

Website: _____
Username: _____
Password: _____
Notes: _____
_____
_____
_____

A
B
C
D
E
F
G
H
I
J
K
L
M
N
O
P
Q
R
S
T
U
V
W
X
Y
Z

A
B  Website: _____
C  Username: _____
D  Password: _____
E  Notes: _____
F  _____
G  _____

H  Website: _____
I  Username: _____
J  Password: _____
K  Notes: _____
L  _____
**M** _____

N  Website: _____
O  Username: _____
P  Password: _____
Q  Notes: _____
R  _____
S  _____
T
U  Website: _____
V  Username: _____
W  Password: _____
X  Notes: _____
Y  _____
Z  _____

Website: _____

Username: _____

Password: _____

Notes: _____

_____

_____

Website: _____

Username: _____

Password: _____

Notes: _____

_____

_____

Website: _____

Username: _____

Password: _____

Notes: _____

_____

_____

Website: _____

Username: _____

Password: _____

Notes: _____

_____

_____

A
B
C
D
E
F
G
H
I
J
K
L
**M**
N
O
P
Q
R
S
T
U
V
W
X
Y
Z

A
B
C
D
E
F
G

Website: _____
Username: _____
Password: _____
Notes: _____
_____
_____

H
I
J
K
L
**M**

Website: _____
Username: _____
Password: _____
Notes: _____
_____
_____

N
O
P
Q
R
S
T

Website: _____
Username: _____
Password: _____
Notes: _____
_____
_____

U
V
W
X
Y
Z

Website: _____
Username: _____
Password: _____
Notes: _____
_____
_____

Website: _____

Username: _____

Password: _____

Notes: _____

_____

_____

Website: _____

Username: _____

Password: _____

Notes: _____

_____

_____

Website: _____

Username: _____

Password: _____

Notes: _____

_____

_____

Website: _____

Username: _____

Password: _____

Notes: _____

_____

_____

A B C D E F G H I J K L M **N** O P Q R S T U V W X Y Z

A
B
C
D
E
F
G
H
I
J
K
L
M
**N**
O
P
Q
R
S
T
U
V
W
X
Y
Z

Website: _____
Username: _____
Password: _____
Notes: _____
_____
_____

Website: _____
Username: _____
Password: _____
Notes: _____
_____
_____

Website: _____
Username: _____
Password: _____
Notes: _____
_____
_____

Website: _____
Username: _____
Password: _____
Notes: _____
_____
_____

Website: _____

Username: _____

Password: _____

Notes: _____

_____

_____

Website: _____

Username: _____

Password: _____

Notes: _____

_____

_____

Website: _____

Username: _____

Password: _____

Notes: _____

_____

_____

Website: _____

Username: _____

Password: _____

Notes: _____

_____

_____

A
B
C
D
E
F
G
H
I
J
K
L
M
N
O
P
Q
R
S
T
U
V
W
X
Y
Z

A B C D E F G H I J K L M **N** O P Q R S T U V W X Y Z

Website: _____

Username: _____

Password: _____

Notes: _____

_____

_____

Website: _____

Username: _____

Password: _____

Notes: _____

_____

_____

Website: _____

Username: _____

Password: _____

Notes: _____

_____

_____

Website: _____

Username: _____

Password: _____

Notes: _____

_____

_____

Website: _____

Username: _____

Password: _____

Notes: _____

_____

_____

Website: _____

Username: _____

Password: _____

Notes: _____

_____

_____

Website: _____

Username: _____

Password: _____

Notes: _____

_____

_____

Website: _____

Username: _____

Password: _____

Notes: _____

_____

_____

A
B
C
D
E
F
G
H
I
J
K
L
M
N
O
P
Q
R
S
T
U
V
W
X
Y
Z

A
B
C
D
E
F
G
H
I
J
K
L
M
N
**O**
P
Q
R
S
T
U
V
W
X
Y
Z

Website: _____
Username: _____
Password: _____
Notes: _____
_____
_____

Website: _____
Username: _____
Password: _____
Notes: _____
_____
_____

Website: _____
Username: _____
Password: _____
Notes: _____
_____
_____

Website: _____
Username: _____
Password: _____
Notes: _____
_____
_____

Website: _____

Username: _____

Password: _____

Notes: _____

_____

_____

Website: _____

Username: _____

Password: _____

Notes: _____

_____

_____

Website: _____

Username: _____

Password: _____

Notes: _____

_____

_____

Website: _____

Username: _____

Password: _____

Notes: _____

_____

_____

A
B
C
D
E
F
G
H
I
J
K
L
M
N
O
P
Q
R
S
T
U
V
W
X
Y
Z

A
B
C
D
E
F
G

Website: _____
Username: _____
Password: _____
Notes: _____

_____

_____

H
I
J
K
L
M

Website: _____
Username: _____
Password: _____
Notes: _____

_____

_____

N
**O**
P
Q
R
S
T

Website: _____
Username: _____
Password: _____
Notes: _____

_____

_____

U
V
W
X
Y
Z

Website: _____
Username: _____
Password: _____
Notes: _____

_____

_____

Website: _____

Username: _____

Password: _____

Notes: _____

_____

_____

Website: _____

Username: _____

Password: _____

Notes: _____

_____

_____

Website: _____

Username: _____

Password: _____

Notes: _____

_____

_____

Website: _____

Username: _____

Password: _____

Notes: _____

_____

_____

A
B
C
D
E
F
G
H
I
J
K
L
M
N
O
**P**
Q
R
S
T
U
V
W
X
Y
Z

A
B
C
D
E
F
G

Website: _____
Username: _____
Password: _____
Notes: _____
_____
_____

H
I
J
K
L
M

Website: _____
Username: _____
Password: _____
Notes: _____
_____
_____

N
O
**P**
Q
R
S
T

Website: _____
Username: _____
Password: _____
Notes: _____
_____
_____

U
V
W
X
Y
Z

Website: _____
Username: _____
Password: _____
Notes: _____
_____
_____

Website: _____

Username: _____

Password: _____

Notes: _____

_____

_____

Website: _____

Username: _____

Password: _____

Notes: _____

_____

_____

Website: _____

Username: _____

Password: _____

Notes: _____

_____

_____

Website: _____

Username: _____

Password: _____

Notes: _____

_____

_____

A
B
C
D
E
F
G
H
I
J
K
L
M
N
O
**P**
Q
R
S
T
U
V
W
X
Y
Z

A
B
C
D
E
F

Website: _____
Username: _____
Password: _____
Notes: _____
_____
_____

G
H
I
J
K
L
M

Website: _____
Username: _____
Password: _____
Notes: _____
_____
_____

N
O
**P**
Q
R
S
T

Website: _____
Username: _____
Password: _____
Notes: _____
_____
_____

U
V
W
X
Y
Z

Website: _____
Username: _____
Password: _____
Notes: _____
_____
_____

Website: _____

Username: _____

Password: _____

Notes: _____

_____

_____

Website: _____

Username: _____

Password: _____

Notes: _____

_____

_____

Website: _____

Username: _____

Password: _____

Notes: _____

_____

_____

Website: _____

Username: _____

Password: _____

Notes: _____

_____

_____

A
B
C
D
E
F
G
H
I
J
K
L
M
N
O
P
**Q**
R
S
T
U
V
W
X
Y
Z

A
B
C
D
E
F
G
H
I
J
K
L
M
N
O
P
**Q**
R
S
T
U
V
W
X
Y
Z

Website: _____
Username: _____
Password: _____
Notes: _____
_____
_____

Website: _____
Username: _____
Password: _____
Notes: _____
_____
_____

Website: _____
Username: _____
Password: _____
Notes: _____
_____
_____

Website: _____
Username: _____
Password: _____
Notes: _____
_____
_____

Website: _____
Username: _____
Password: _____
Notes: _____
_____
_____

Website: _____
Username: _____
Password: _____
Notes: _____
_____
_____

Website: _____
Username: _____
Password: _____
Notes: _____
_____
_____

Website: _____
Username: _____
Password: _____
Notes: _____
_____
_____

A
B
C
D
E
F
G
H
I
J
K
L
M
N
O
P
**Q**
R
S
T
U
V
W
X
Y
Z

A
B
C
D
E
F
G

Website: _____
Username: _____
Password: _____
Notes: _____
_____
_____

H
I
J
K
L
M

Website: _____
Username: _____
Password: _____
Notes: _____
_____
_____

N
O
P
**Q**
R
S
T

Website: _____
Username: _____
Password: _____
Notes: _____
_____
_____

U
V
W
X
Y
Z

Website: _____
Username: _____
Password: _____
Notes: _____
_____
_____

Website: _____
Username: _____
Password: _____
Notes: _____
_____
_____

Website: _____
Username: _____
Password: _____
Notes: _____
_____
_____

Website: _____
Username: _____
Password: _____
Notes: _____
_____
_____

Website: _____
Username: _____
Password: _____
Notes: _____
_____
_____

A
B
C
D
E
F
G
H
I
J
K
L
M
N
O
P
Q
**R**
S
T
U
V
W
X
Y
Z

A
B
C
D
E
F
G

Website: _____
Username: _____
Password: _____
Notes: _____
_____
_____

H
I
J
K
L
M
N

Website: _____
Username: _____
Password: _____
Notes: _____
_____
_____

O
P
Q
**R**
S
T

Website: _____
Username: _____
Password: _____
Notes: _____
_____
_____

U
V
W
X
Y
Z

Website: _____
Username: _____
Password: _____
Notes: _____
_____
_____

Website: _____

Username: _____

Password: _____

Notes: _____

_____

_____

Website: _____

Username: _____

Password: _____

Notes: _____

_____

_____

Website: _____

Username: _____

Password: _____

Notes: _____

_____

_____

Website: _____

Username: _____

Password: _____

Notes: _____

_____

_____

A
B
C
D
E
F
G
H
I
J
K
L
M
N
O
P
Q
**R**
S
T
U
V
W
X
Y
Z

A
B Website: _____
C Username: _____
D Password: _____
E Notes: _____
F _____
G _____

H Website: _____
I Username: _____
J Password: _____
K Notes: _____
L _____
M _____

N Website: _____
O Username: _____
P Password: _____
Q Notes: _____
**R** _____
S _____

T Website: _____
U Username: _____
V Password: _____
W Notes: _____
X _____
Y _____
Z

Website: _____

Username: _____

Password: _____

Notes: _____

_____

_____

Website: _____

Username: _____

Password: _____

Notes: _____

_____

_____

Website: _____

Username: _____

Password: _____

Notes: _____

_____

_____

Website: _____

Username: _____

Password: _____

Notes: _____

_____

_____

A
B
C
D
E
F
G
H
I
J
K
L
M
N
O
P
Q
R
S
T
U
V
W
X
Y
Z

A
B          Website: _____
           Username: _____
C          Password: _____
D          Notes: _____
E          _____
F          _____
G
H          Website: _____
           Username: _____
I
J          Password: _____
           Notes: _____
K
L          _____
M          _____
N          Website: _____
O          Username: _____
P          Password: _____
Q          Notes: _____
R          _____
**S**      _____
T
U          Website: _____
           Username: _____
V          Password: _____
W          Notes: _____
X
Y          _____
           _____
Z

Website: _____

Username: _____

Password: _____

Notes: _____

_____

_____

Website: _____

Username: _____

Password: _____

Notes: _____

_____

_____

Website: _____

Username: _____

Password: _____

Notes: _____

_____

_____

Website: _____

Username: _____

Password: _____

Notes: _____

_____

_____

A
B
C
D
E
F
G
H
I
J
K
L
M
N
O
P
Q
R
**S**
T
U
V
W
X
Y
Z

A
B
C
D
E
F
G

Website: _____
Username: _____
Password: _____
Notes: _____
_____
_____

H
I
J
K
L
M

Website: _____
Username: _____
Password: _____
Notes: _____
_____
_____

N
O
P
Q
R
**S**
T

Website: _____
Username: _____
Password: _____
Notes: _____
_____
_____

U
V
W
X
Y
Z

Website: _____
Username: _____
Password: _____
Notes: _____
_____
_____

Website: _____

Username: _____

Password: _____

Notes: _____

_____

_____

_____

Website: _____

Username: _____

Password: _____

Notes: _____

_____

_____

_____

Website: _____

Username: _____

Password: _____

Notes: _____

_____

_____

_____

Website: _____

Username: _____

Password: _____

Notes: _____

_____

_____

A
B
C
D
E
F
G
H
I
J
K
L
M
N
O
P
Q
R
S
**T**
U
V
W
X
Y
Z

A
B
C
D
E
F

Website: _____
Username: _____
Password: _____
Notes: _____
_____
_____

G
H
I
J
K
L
M

Website: _____
Username: _____
Password: _____
Notes: _____
_____
_____

N
O
P
Q
R
S

Website: _____
Username: _____
Password: _____
Notes: _____
_____
_____

**T**
U
V
W
X
Y
Z

Website: _____
Username: _____
Password: _____
Notes: _____
_____
_____

Website: _____

Username: _____

Password: _____

Notes: _____

_____

_____

Website: _____

Username: _____

Password: _____

Notes: _____

_____

_____

Website: _____

Username: _____

Password: _____

Notes: _____

_____

_____

Website: _____

Username: _____

Password: _____

Notes: _____

_____

_____

A
B
C
D
E
F
G
H
I
J
K
L
M
N
O
P
Q
R
S
T
U
V
W
X
Y
Z

A
B
C
D
E
F

Website: _____
Username: _____
Password: _____
Notes: _____
_____
_____

G
H
I
J
K
L
M

Website: _____
Username: _____
Password: _____
Notes: _____
_____
_____

N
O
P
Q
R
S

Website: _____
Username: _____
Password: _____
Notes: _____
_____
_____

**T**
U
V
W
X
Y
Z

Website: _____
Username: _____
Password: _____
Notes: _____
_____
_____

Website: _____
Username: _____
Password: _____
Notes: _____
_____
_____

Website: _____
Username: _____
Password: _____
Notes: _____
_____
_____

Website: _____
Username: _____
Password: _____
Notes: _____
_____
_____

Website: _____
Username: _____
Password: _____
Notes: _____
_____
_____

A
B
C
D
E
F
G
H
I
J
K
L
M
N
O
P
Q
R
S
T
U
V
W
X
Y
Z

A
B
C
D
E
F
G

Website: _____
Username: _____
Password: _____
Notes: _____
_____
_____

H
I
J
K
L
M

Website: _____
Username: _____
Password: _____
Notes: _____
_____
_____

N
O
P
Q
R
S
T

Website: _____
Username: _____
Password: _____
Notes: _____
_____
_____

**U**

Website: _____
Username: _____
Password: _____
Notes: _____
_____
_____

V
W
X
Y
Z

Website: _____

Username: _____

Password: _____

Notes: _____

_____

_____

_____

Website: _____

Username: _____

Password: _____

Notes: _____

_____

_____

_____

Website: _____

Username: _____

Password: _____

Notes: _____

_____

_____

_____

Website: _____

Username: _____

Password: _____

Notes: _____

_____

_____

A
B
C
D
E
F
G
H
I
J
K
L
M
N
O
P
Q
R
S
T
**U**
V
W
X
Y
Z

A
B Website: _____
C Username: _____
  Password: _____
D Notes: _____
E _____
F _____
G _____
H Website: _____
I Username: _____
  Password: _____
J Notes: _____
K
L _____
M _____
N _____
O Website: _____
  Username: _____
P Password: _____
Q Notes: _____
R
S _____
T _____
U Website: _____
  Username: _____
V Password: _____
W Notes: _____
X
Y _____
Z _____

Website: _____

Username: _____

Password: _____

Notes: _____

_____

_____

Website: _____

Username: _____

Password: _____

Notes: _____

_____

_____

Website: _____

Username: _____

Password: _____

Notes: _____

_____

_____

Website: _____

Username: _____

Password: _____

Notes: _____

_____

_____

A
B
C
D
E
F
G
H
I
J
K
L
M
N
O
P
Q
R
S
T
U
**V**
W
X
Y
Z

A
B
C
D
E
F

Website: _____
Username: _____
Password: _____
Notes: _____
_____
_____

G
H
I
J
K
L
M

Website: _____
Username: _____
Password: _____
Notes: _____
_____
_____

N
O
P
Q
R
S
T

Website: _____
Username: _____
Password: _____
Notes: _____
_____
_____

U
**V**
W
X
Y
Z

Website: _____
Username: _____
Password: _____
Notes: _____
_____
_____

Website: _____

Username: _____

Password: _____

Notes: _____

_____

_____

Website: _____

Username: _____

Password: _____

Notes: _____

_____

_____

Website: _____

Username: _____

Password: _____

Notes: _____

_____

_____

Website: _____

Username: _____

Password: _____

Notes: _____

_____

_____

A
B
C
D
E
F
G
H
I
J
K
L
M
N
O
P
Q
R
S
T
U
**V**
W
X
Y
Z

A
B
C
D
E
F
G
H
I
J
K
L
M
N
O
P
Q
R
S
T
U
**V**
W
X
Y
Z

Website: _____
Username: _____
Password: _____
Notes: _____
_____
_____

Website: _____
Username: _____
Password: _____
Notes: _____
_____
_____

Website: _____
Username: _____
Password: _____
Notes: _____
_____
_____

Website: _____
Username: _____
Password: _____
Notes: _____
_____
_____

Website: _____

Username: _____

Password: _____

Notes: _____

_____

_____

_____

Website: _____

Username: _____

Password: _____

Notes: _____

_____

_____

_____

Website: _____

Username: _____

Password: _____

Notes: _____

_____

_____

_____

Website: _____

Username: _____

Password: _____

Notes: _____

_____

_____

A
B
C
D
E
F
G
H
I
J
K
L
M
N
O
P
Q
R
S
T
U
V
**W**
X
Y
Z

A
B
C
D
E
F
G
H
I
J
K
L
M
N
O
P
Q
R
S
T
U
V
**W**
X
Y
Z

Website: _____

Username: _____

Password: _____

Notes: _____

_____

_____

Website: _____

Username: _____

Password: _____

Notes: _____

_____

_____

Website: _____

Username: _____

Password: _____

Notes: _____

_____

_____

Website: _____

Username: _____

Password: _____

Notes: _____

_____

_____

Website: _____

Username: _____

Password: _____

Notes: _____

_____

_____

Website: _____

Username: _____

Password: _____

Notes: _____

_____

_____

Website: _____

Username: _____

Password: _____

Notes: _____

_____

_____

Website: _____

Username: _____

Password: _____

Notes: _____

_____

_____

A
B
C
D
E
F
G
H
I
J
K
L
M
N
O
P
Q
R
S
T
U
V
**W**
X
Y
Z

A
B
C
D
E
F

Website: _____
Username: _____
Password: _____
Notes: _____
_____
_____

G
H
I
J
K
L
M

Website: _____
Username: _____
Password: _____
Notes: _____
_____
_____

N
O
P
Q
R
S
T

Website: _____
Username: _____
Password: _____
Notes: _____
_____
_____

U
V
**W**
X
Y
Z

Website: _____
Username: _____
Password: _____
Notes: _____
_____
_____

Website: _____

Username: _____

Password: _____

Notes: _____

_____

_____

Website: _____

Username: _____

Password: _____

Notes: _____

_____

_____

Website: _____

Username: _____

Password: _____

Notes: _____

_____

_____

Website: _____

Username: _____

Password: _____

Notes: _____

_____

_____

A
B
C
D
E
F
G
H
I
J
K
L
M
N
O
P
Q
R
S
T
U
V
W
X
Y
Z

A
B
C
D
E
F
G

Website: _____
Username: _____
Password: _____
Notes: _____
_____
_____
_____

H
I
J
K
L
M

Website: _____
Username: _____
Password: _____
Notes: _____
_____
_____
_____

N
O
P
Q
R
S
T

Website: _____
Username: _____
Password: _____
Notes: _____
_____
_____
_____

U
V
W
**X**
Y
Z

Website: _____
Username: _____
Password: _____
Notes: _____
_____
_____

Website: _____

Username: _____

Password: _____

Notes: _____

_____

_____

Website: _____

Username: _____

Password: _____

Notes: _____

_____

_____

Website: _____

Username: _____

Password: _____

Notes: _____

_____

_____

Website: _____

Username: _____

Password: _____

Notes: _____

_____

_____

A
B
C
D
E
F
G
H
I
J
K
L
M
N
O
P
Q
R
S
T
U
V
W
X
Y
Z

A
B
C
D
E
F
G
H
I
J
K
L
M
N
O
P
Q
R
S
T
U
V
W
**X**
Y
Z

Website: _____

Username: _____

Password: _____

Notes: _____

_____

_____

Website: _____

Username: _____

Password: _____

Notes: _____

_____

_____

Website: _____

Username: _____

Password: _____

Notes: _____

_____

_____

Website: _____

Username: _____

Password: _____

Notes: _____

_____

_____

Website: _____

Username: _____

Password: _____

Notes: _____

_____

_____

Website: _____

Username: _____

Password: _____

Notes: _____

_____

_____

Website: _____

Username: _____

Password: _____

Notes: _____

_____

_____

Website: _____

Username: _____

Password: _____

Notes: _____

_____

_____

A
B
C
D
E
F
G
H
I
J
K
L
M
N
O
P
Q
R
S
T
U
V
W
X
**Y**
Z

A
B
C
D
E
F
G
H
I
J
K
L
M
N
O
P
Q
R
S
T
U
V
W
X
**Y**
Z

Website: _____
Username: _____
Password: _____
Notes: _____
_____
_____

Website: _____
Username: _____
Password: _____
Notes: _____
_____
_____

Website: _____
Username: _____
Password: _____
Notes: _____
_____
_____

Website: _____
Username: _____
Password: _____
Notes: _____
_____
_____

Website: _____

Username: _____

Password: _____

Notes: _____

_____

_____

Website: _____

Username: _____

Password: _____

Notes: _____

_____

_____

Website: _____

Username: _____

Password: _____

Notes: _____

_____

_____

Website: _____

Username: _____

Password: _____

Notes: _____

_____

_____

A
B
C
D
E
F
G
H
I
J
K
L
M
N
O
P
Q
R
S
T
U
V
W
X
**Y**
Z

A
B
C
D
E
F
G
H
I
J
K
L
M
N
O
P
Q
R
S
T
U
V
W
X
**Y**
Z

Website: _____

Username: _____

Password: _____

Notes: _____

_____

_____

Website: _____

Username: _____

Password: _____

Notes: _____

_____

_____

Website: _____

Username: _____

Password: _____

Notes: _____

_____

_____

Website: _____

Username: _____

Password: _____

Notes: _____

_____

_____

Website: _____

Username: _____

Password: _____

Notes: _____

_____

_____

Website: _____

Username: _____

Password: _____

Notes: _____

_____

_____

Website: _____

Username: _____

Password: _____

Notes: _____

_____

_____

Website: _____

Username: _____

Password: _____

Notes: _____

_____

_____

A
B
C
D
E
F
G
H
I
J
K
L
M
N
O
P
Q
R
S
T
U
V
W
X
Y
**Z**

A
B
C
D
E
F
G

Website: _____
Username: _____
Password: _____
Notes: _____
_____
_____

H
I
J
K
L
M

Website: _____
Username: _____
Password: _____
Notes: _____
_____
_____

N
O
P
Q
R
S
T

Website: _____
Username: _____
Password: _____
Notes: _____
_____
_____

U
V
W
X
Y
Z

Website: _____
Username: _____
Password: _____
Notes: _____
_____
_____

Website: _____

Username: _____

Password: _____

Notes: _____

_____

_____

Website: _____

Username: _____

Password: _____

Notes: _____

_____

_____

Website: _____

Username: _____

Password: _____

Notes: _____

_____

_____

Website: _____

Username: _____

Password: _____

Notes: _____

_____

_____

A
B
C
D
E
F
G
H
I
J
K
L
M
N
O
P
Q
R
S
T
U
V
W
X
Y
Z

A
B
C
D
E
F
G

Website: _____
Username: _____
Password: _____
Notes: _____
_____
_____

H
I
J
K
L
M

Website: _____
Username: _____
Password: _____
Notes: _____
_____
_____

N
O
P
Q
R
S
T

Website: _____
Username: _____
Password: _____
Notes: _____
_____
_____

U
V
W
X
Y
Z

Website: _____
Username: _____
Password: _____
Notes: _____
_____
_____

# Notes

# Notes

# Notes

# Notes

# Notes

# Notes

# Notes

# Notes

# Notes

# Notes

# Notes

# Notes

# Notes

# Notes

69165076R00071